Created, published, and distributed by Knock Knock
6080 Center Drive
Los Angeles, CA 90045
knockknockstuff.com
Knock Knock is a registered trademark of Knock Knock LLC
Inner-Truth is a registered trademark of Knock Knock LLC

ISBN: 978-160106928-3
UPC: 825703-50145-2

10 9

A GRATITUDE JOURNAL? REALLY?

IT'S NOT ENOUGH TO SAY THANK YOU— NOW I HAVE TO WRITE IT DOWN IN A BOOK?

Isn't this a little woo-woo, a little self-helpy, a little too trite? Is this really the path to happiness? If you're looking for a way to develop a more positive attitude, to be happier, healthier, and more at peace in your life, you're certainly not alone. As many have discovered before you, a gratitude journal is an effective way to start. No matter how cheesy it sounds, a gratitude journal is truly good for your mental and physical health. There's even a lot of science behind it. It is good to be grateful, but it's even better to write it down.

The Greater Good Science Center at UC Berkeley has made an extensive study of gratitude, and is a big promoter of gratitude journals. "As we've reported many times over the years, studies have traced a range of impressive benefits to the simple act of writing down the things for which we're grateful—benefits including better sleep, fewer symptoms of illness, and more happiness among adults and kids alike." More specifically, the benefits of gratitude cited include "stronger immune systems and lower blood pressure, higher levels of positive emotions, more joy, optimism, and happiness, acting with more generosity and compassion, feeling less lonely and isolated." That all sounds pretty darn good.

The American Psychological Association published a report showing evidence that expressing gratitude can result in "improved mental, and ultimately physical, health in patients with asymptomatic heart failure." According to lead author Paul J. Mills, PhD, "It seems that a more grateful heart is indeed a more healthy heart, and that gratitude journaling is an easy way to support cardiac health." Suffice it to say, the benefits of gratitude, and of expressing it in a journal, are very real. Not woo-woo at all.

The science behind gratitude journals dovetails nicely with the science behind journaling in general. According to a widely cited study by James W. Pennebaker and Janel D. Seagal, "Writing about important personal experiences in an emotional way...brings about improvements in mental and physical health." Proven benefits include better stress management, strengthened immune systems, fewer doctor visits, and improvement in chronic illnesses such as asthma.

It's not entirely clear how journaling accomplishes all this. Catharsis is involved, but many also point to the value of organizing experiences into a cohesive narrative. According to *Newsweek*, some experts believe that journaling "forces us to transform the ruminations cluttering our minds into coherent stories."

To get the most of the journaling process, here are a few tips. Specialists agree you should try to write, quasi-daily, for at least 5–15 minutes. If you find yourself unable to muster a positive thought, don't stress. Instead, use the quotes inside this journal as a jumping-off point for observations and explorations. Don't critique your writing, just spew. Finally, choose a home for your journal where others can't find it.

Positive is good. Think of the beautiful and kind things you experienced during your day: the delicious, the fragrant, the sensual. If need be, you can also approach gratitude from a negative perspective. "I'm grateful that I didn't shove my shopping cart into the idiot taking up all that room in the gluten-free section" is still gratitude. You can even curse! In fact, there may be a day when swearing is what you're most grateful for. Can't think of anything? Go with the basics. You're alive. Your brain works. There may be something good in the fridge. There's something decent on TV. These may not be exciting, but they are important.

The goal is to pay more attention and find gratitude across the spectrum of your daily life, the tiny things and the major events. As the folks at the Greater Good Science Center observe, "keeping a gratitude journal—or perhaps the entire experience of gratitude—is really about forcing ourselves to pay attention to the good things in life we'd otherwise take for granted."

My expectations were reduced to zero when I was 21. Everything since then has been a bonus.

Stephen Hawking

DATE

WHY I'M GRATEFUL TODAY, MORE OR LESS:

TODAY'S GRATITUDE LEVEL:

All sanity depends on this: that it should be a delight to feel the roughness of a carpet under smooth soles, a delight to feel heat strike the skin, a delight to stand upright, knowing the bones are moving easily under the flesh.

Doris Lessing

DATE

WHY I'M GRATEFUL TODAY, MORE OR LESS:

TODAY'S GRATITUDE LEVEL:

In the midst of winter, I finally learned that there was in me an invincible summer.

Albert Camus

DATE

WHY I'M GRATEFUL TODAY, MORE OR LESS:

TODAY'S GRATITUDE LEVEL:

Some people grumble
that roses have thorns;
I am grateful that
thorns have roses.

Alphonse Karr

DATE

WHY I'M GRATEFUL TODAY, MORE OR LESS:

TODAY'S GRATITUDE LEVEL:

I think I'm the happiest I've ever been. Part of it is just learning what makes me happier and doing more of it, and learning what makes me unhappier and doing less of it.

Mark Frauenfelder

DATE

WHY I'M GRATEFUL TODAY, MORE OR LESS:

TODAY'S GRATITUDE LEVEL:

For after all, the best
thing one can do
When it is raining,
is to let it rain.

Henry Wadsworth Longfellow

DATE

WHY I'M GRATEFUL TODAY, MORE OR LESS:

TODAY'S GRATITUDE LEVEL:

When all else fails, you always have delusion.

Conan O'Brien

DATE

WHY I'M GRATEFUL TODAY, MORE OR LESS:

TODAY'S GRATITUDE LEVEL:

If you observe a really happy man, you will find him building a boat, writing a symphony, educating his son, growing double dahlias in his garden, or looking for dinosaur eggs in the Gobi desert. He will not be searching for happiness as if it were a collar button that has rolled under the radiator.

W. Béran Wolfe

DATE

WHY I'M GRATEFUL TODAY, MORE OR LESS:

TODAY'S GRATITUDE LEVEL:

Life is a spell so exquisite that everything conspires to break it.

Emily Dickinson

DATE

WHY I'M GRATEFUL TODAY, MORE OR LESS:

TODAY'S GRATITUDE LEVEL:

Got no checkbooks, got no banks, /
Still I'd like to express my thanks— /
I got the sun in the morning /
And the moon at night.

Irving Berlin

DATE

WHY I'M GRATEFUL TODAY, MORE OR LESS:

TODAY'S GRATITUDE LEVEL:

Thankfully, dreams can change. If we'd all stuck with our first dream, the world would be overrun with cowboys and princesses.

Stephen Colbert

DATE

WHY I'M GRATEFUL TODAY, MORE OR LESS:

TODAY'S GRATITUDE LEVEL:

It's never too late to have a happy childhood.

Tom Robbins

DATE

WHY I'M GRATEFUL TODAY, MORE OR LESS:

TODAY'S GRATITUDE LEVEL:

Let us be thankful for the fools. But for them the rest of us could not succeed.

Mark Twain

DATE

WHY I'M GRATEFUL TODAY, MORE OR LESS:

TODAY'S GRATITUDE LEVEL:

I've endured a few knocks
but missed worse. I know
how lucky I am, and secretly
tap wood, greet the day, and
grab a sneaky pleasure from
my survival at long odds.

Roger Angell

DATE

WHY I'M GRATEFUL TODAY, MORE OR LESS:

TODAY'S GRATITUDE LEVEL:

How lucky I am
to have something
that makes saying
goodbye so hard.

A. A. Milne

DATE

WHY I'M GRATEFUL TODAY, MORE OR LESS:

TODAY'S GRATITUDE LEVEL:

Appreciation is like an insurance policy. It has to be renewed every now and then.

Dave McIntyre

DATE

WHY I'M GRATEFUL TODAY, MORE OR LESS:

TODAY'S GRATITUDE LEVEL:

The hardest arithmetic to master is that which enables us to count our blessings.

Eric Hoffer

DATE

WHY I'M GRATEFUL TODAY, MORE OR LESS:

TODAY'S GRATITUDE LEVEL:

I’m so glad cities have personalities, just like people have personalities. That’s something that makes me smile.

Fred Armisen

DATE

WHY I'M GRATEFUL TODAY, MORE OR LESS:

TODAY'S GRATITUDE LEVEL:

They both seemed to understand that describing it was beyond their powers, the gratitude that spreads through your body when a burden gets lifted, and the sense of homecoming that follows, when you suddenly remember what it feels like to be yourself.

Tom Perrotta

DATE

WHY I'M GRATEFUL TODAY, MORE OR LESS:

TODAY'S GRATITUDE LEVEL:

This is a wonderful day. I've never seen this one before.

Maya Angelou

DATE

WHY I'M GRATEFUL TODAY, MORE OR LESS:

TODAY'S GRATITUDE LEVEL:

You never know what worse luck your bad luck has saved you from.

Cormac McCarthy

DATE

WHY I'M GRATEFUL TODAY, MORE OR LESS:

TODAY'S GRATITUDE LEVEL:

The artist is extremely lucky who is presented with the worst possible ordeal which will not actually kill him. At that point, he's in business: Beethoven's deafness, Goya's deafness, Milton's blindness, that kind of thing.

John Berryman

WHY I'M GRATEFUL TODAY, MORE OR LESS:

TODAY'S GRATITUDE LEVEL:

Walk as if you are kissing the Earth with your feet.

Thich Nhat Hanh

DATE

WHY I'M GRATEFUL TODAY, MORE OR LESS:

TODAY'S GRATITUDE LEVEL:

Joy is what happens when we allow ourselves to recognize how good things are.

Marianne Williamson

DATE

WHY I'M GRATEFUL TODAY, MORE OR LESS:

TODAY'S GRATITUDE LEVEL:

Developing an adequate response to rejection, neither defensive nor sentimental, lies at the heart of any serious attempt at sanity.

Alain de Botton

DATE

WHY I'M GRATEFUL TODAY, MORE OR LESS:

TODAY'S GRATITUDE LEVEL:

Aside from purely technical analysis, nothing can be *said* about music, except when it is bad; when it is good, one can only listen and be grateful.

W. H. Auden

DATE

WHY I'M GRATEFUL TODAY, MORE OR LESS:

TODAY'S GRATITUDE LEVEL:

Unexpected intrusions of beauty. This is what life is.

Saul Bellow

DATE

WHY I'M GRATEFUL TODAY, MORE OR LESS:

TODAY'S GRATITUDE LEVEL:

What robe can Gratitude employ
So seemly as the radiant vest of Joy?

William Wordsworth

DATE

WHY I'M GRATEFUL TODAY, MORE OR LESS:

TODAY'S GRATITUDE LEVEL:

Delicious autumn!
My very soul is wedded
to it, and if I were a
bird I would fly about
the earth seeking the
successive autumns.

George Eliot

DATE

WHY I'M GRATEFUL TODAY, MORE OR LESS:

TODAY'S GRATITUDE LEVEL:

For me, peace comes when I . . . embrace the beautiful mess that I am, and embrace the beautiful mess that you all are, and that this world is. And just let it be that.

Elizabeth Gilbert

DATE

WHY I'M GRATEFUL TODAY, MORE OR LESS:

TODAY'S GRATITUDE LEVEL:

Maybe the only thing worse than having to give gratitude constantly all the time, is having to accept it.

William Faulkner

DATE

WHY I'M GRATEFUL TODAY, MORE OR LESS:

TODAY'S GRATITUDE LEVEL:

I thank God for my failures. Maybe not at the time, but after some reflection. I never feel like a failure just because something I tried has failed.

Dolly Parton

DATE

WHY I'M GRATEFUL TODAY, MORE OR LESS:

TODAY'S GRATITUDE LEVEL:

The great flood-gates of the wonder-world swung open.

Herman Melville

DATE

WHY I'M GRATEFUL TODAY, MORE OR LESS:

TODAY'S GRATITUDE LEVEL:

Consider the possibility that
you might actually be lucky
when you get rejected from stuff.
Because of this streak of what
appeared to be bad luck, I fell into
my life as it is today.

Lisa Yuskavage

DATE

WHY I'M GRATEFUL TODAY, MORE OR LESS:

TODAY'S GRATITUDE LEVEL:

Taking the long view, I'm thankful that we're no longer hunter-gatherers, which has certainly freed up some time.

Paula Poundstone

DATE

WHY I'M GRATEFUL TODAY, MORE OR LESS:

TODAY'S GRATITUDE LEVEL:

I love the Sunday Morning. I hail it from afar. I wake with gladness & a holiday feeling always on that day.

Ralph Waldo Emerson

DATE

WHY I'M GRATEFUL TODAY, MORE OR LESS:

TODAY'S GRATITUDE LEVEL:

Luckily, I'm blessed with a well-developed sense of absurdity—it's what saved me.

John Baldessari

DATE

WHY I'M GRATEFUL TODAY, MORE OR LESS:

TODAY'S GRATITUDE LEVEL:

When I started counting my blessings, my whole life turned around.

Willie Nelson

DATE

WHY I'M GRATEFUL TODAY, MORE OR LESS:

TODAY'S GRATITUDE LEVEL:

Thank you India /
Thank you terror /
Thank you disillusionment /
Thank you frailty /
Thank you consequence /
Thank you thank you silence

Alanis Morissette

DATE

WHY I'M GRATEFUL TODAY, MORE OR LESS:

TODAY'S GRATITUDE LEVEL:

I urge you to please notice when you are happy, and exclaim or murmur or think at some point, "If this isn't nice, I don't know what is."

Kurt Vonnegut

DATE

WHY I'M GRATEFUL TODAY, MORE OR LESS:

TODAY'S GRATITUDE LEVEL:

Not because of victories
I sing,
having none,
but for the common sunshine,
the breeze,
the largess of the spring.

Charles Reznikoff

DATE

WHY I'M GRATEFUL TODAY, MORE OR LESS:

TODAY'S GRATITUDE LEVEL:

I love New York on summer afternoons when everyone's away. There's something very sensuous about it—overripe, as if all sorts of funny fruits were going to fall into your hands.

F. Scott Fitzgerald

DATE

WHY I'M GRATEFUL TODAY, MORE OR LESS:

TODAY'S GRATITUDE LEVEL:

Two roads diverged in a wood, and I—
I took the one less traveled by,
And that has made all the difference.

Robert Frost

DATE

WHY I'M GRATEFUL TODAY, MORE OR LESS:

TODAY'S GRATITUDE LEVEL:

When we lose one blessing, another is often most unexpectedly given in its place.

C. S. Lewis

DATE

WHY I'M GRATEFUL TODAY, MORE OR LESS:

TODAY'S GRATITUDE LEVEL:

There's no place like home!

Dorothy Gale, *The Wizard of Oz*

DATE

WHY I'M GRATEFUL TODAY, MORE OR LESS:

TODAY'S GRATITUDE LEVEL:

I see skies of blue, clouds of white /
The bright blessed day,
the dark sacred night /
And I think to myself /
What a wonderful world.

Louis Armstrong

DATE

WHY I'M GRATEFUL TODAY, MORE OR LESS:

TODAY'S GRATITUDE LEVEL:

If we had no winter, the spring would not be so pleasant.

Anne Bradstreet

DATE

WHY I'M GRATEFUL TODAY, MORE OR LESS:

TODAY'S GRATITUDE LEVEL:

Everything that happens, including humiliations, embarrassments, misfortunes, all has been given like clay, like material for one's art. One must accept it.

Jorge Luis Borges

DATE

WHY I'M GRATEFUL TODAY, MORE OR LESS:

TODAY'S GRATITUDE LEVEL:

Oh, earth, you're too wonderful for anyone to realize you!

Thornton Wilder

DATE

WHY I'M GRATEFUL TODAY, MORE OR LESS:

TODAY'S GRATITUDE LEVEL:

A morning-glory at my window satisfies me more than the metaphysics of books.

Walt Whitman

DATE

WHY I'M GRATEFUL TODAY, MORE OR LESS:

TODAY'S GRATITUDE LEVEL:

As we express our gratitude, we must never forget that the highest appreciation is not to utter words but to live by them.

John F. Kennedy

DATE

WHY I'M GRATEFUL TODAY, MORE OR LESS:

TODAY'S GRATITUDE LEVEL:

Art Is One of Life's Richest Offerings. For those who have not the talent to create, there is appreciation.

Nathanael West

DATE

WHY I'M GRATEFUL TODAY, MORE OR LESS:

TODAY'S GRATITUDE LEVEL:

Reflect upon your present blessings—of which every man has many—not on your past misfortunes, of which all men have some.

Charles Dickens

DATE

WHY I'M GRATEFUL TODAY, MORE OR LESS:

TODAY'S GRATITUDE LEVEL:

There were two ways to be happy: improve your reality, or lower your expectations.

Jodi Picoult

DATE

WHY I'M GRATEFUL TODAY, MORE OR LESS:

TODAY'S GRATITUDE LEVEL:

Not only has Harvard given
me an extraordinary honour,
but the weeks of fear and nausea
I have endured at the thought
of giving this commencement
address have made me lose weight.
A win-win situation!

J. K. Rowling

DATE

WHY I'M GRATEFUL TODAY, MORE OR LESS:

TODAY'S GRATITUDE LEVEL:

If more of us valued food and cheer and song above hoarded gold, it would be a merrier world.

J. R. R. Tolkien

DATE

WHY I'M GRATEFUL TODAY, MORE OR LESS:

TODAY'S GRATITUDE LEVEL:

No one is as capable of gratitude as one who has emerged from the kingdom of night.

Elie Wiesel

DATE

WHY I'M GRATEFUL TODAY, MORE OR LESS:

TODAY'S GRATITUDE LEVEL:

I believe in looking reality straight in the eye and denying it.

Garrison Keillor

DATE

WHY I'M GRATEFUL TODAY, MORE OR LESS:

TODAY'S GRATITUDE LEVEL:

There is no excess in the world so commendable as excessive gratitude.

Jean de La Bruyère

DATE

WHY I'M GRATEFUL TODAY, MORE OR LESS:

TODAY'S GRATITUDE LEVEL:

Live on, survive, for the earth gives forth wonders. It may swallow your heart, but the wonders keep on coming.

Salman Rushdie

WHY I'M GRATEFUL TODAY, MORE OR LESS:

TODAY'S GRATITUDE LEVEL:

Unless you have been
to boarding-school when
you are very young, it is
absolutely impossible to
appreciate the delights
of living at home.

Roald Dahl

DATE

WHY I'M GRATEFUL TODAY, MORE OR LESS:

TODAY'S GRATITUDE LEVEL:

And, in the very room in which he sat, there were books that could take you anywhere, and things to invent, and make, and build, and break, and all the puzzle and excitement of everything he didn't know—music to play, songs to sing, and worlds to imagine and then someday make real.

Norton Juster

DATE

WHY I'M GRATEFUL TODAY, MORE OR LESS:

TODAY'S GRATITUDE LEVEL:

Doing beautiful things is its own reward.

Teller

DATE

WHY I'M GRATEFUL TODAY, MORE OR LESS:

TODAY'S GRATITUDE LEVEL:

A leaf fluttered in through
the window this morning, as if
supported by the rays of the sun,
a bird settled on the fire escape,
joy in the task of coffee, joy
accompanied me as I walked . . .

Anaïs Nin

DATE

WHY I'M GRATEFUL TODAY, MORE OR LESS:

TODAY'S GRATITUDE LEVEL:

Appreciate everything, including the ordinary.

Pema Chödrön

DATE

WHY I'M GRATEFUL TODAY, MORE OR LESS:

TODAY'S GRATITUDE LEVEL:

Trying to be happy by accumulating possessions is like trying to satisfy hunger by taping sandwiches all over my body.

Roger Corless

DATE

WHY I'M GRATEFUL TODAY, MORE OR LESS:

TODAY'S GRATITUDE LEVEL:

Anything one does every day
is important and imposing and
anywhere one lives is interesting
and beautiful.

Gertrude Stein

DATE

WHY I'M GRATEFUL TODAY, MORE OR LESS:

TODAY'S GRATITUDE LEVEL:

Someone I loved once
gave me a box full
of darkness.

It took me years to
understand that this,
too, was a gift.

Mary Oliver

DATE

WHY I'M GRATEFUL TODAY, MORE OR LESS:

TODAY'S GRATITUDE LEVEL:

Say thank you, until you mean it. If you say it long enough, you will believe it.

Melody Beattie

DATE

WHY I'M GRATEFUL TODAY, MORE OR LESS:

TODAY'S GRATITUDE LEVEL:

If we magnified blessings as much as we magnify disappointments, we would all be much happier.

John Wooden

DATE

WHY I'M GRATEFUL TODAY, MORE OR LESS:

TODAY'S GRATITUDE LEVEL:

Every time I see the bumper sticker that says "We think we're humans having spiritual experiences, but we're really spirits having human experiences," I (a) think it's true and (b) want to ram the car.

Anne Lamott

DATE

WHY I'M GRATEFUL TODAY, MORE OR LESS:

TODAY'S GRATITUDE LEVEL:

One of the keys to happiness is a bad memory.

Rita Mae Brown

DATE

WHY I'M GRATEFUL TODAY, MORE OR LESS:

TODAY'S GRATITUDE LEVEL:

So, this is my life. And I want you to know that I am both happy and sad and I'm still trying to figure out how that could be.

Stephen Chbosky

DATE

WHY I'M GRATEFUL TODAY, MORE OR LESS:

TODAY'S GRATITUDE LEVEL:

Let other pens dwell
on guilt and misery.

Jane Austen

DATE

WHY I'M GRATEFUL TODAY, MORE OR LESS:

TODAY'S GRATITUDE LEVEL:

Any happiness you get you've got to make yourself.

Alice Walker

DATE

WHY I'M GRATEFUL TODAY, MORE OR LESS:

TODAY'S GRATITUDE LEVEL:

It is a blessing to get old. It is a blessing to find the time to do the things, to read the books, to listen to the music.

Maurice Sendak

DATE

WHY I'M GRATEFUL TODAY, MORE OR LESS:

TODAY'S GRATITUDE LEVEL:

Gratitude is happiness doubled by wonder.

G. K. Chesterton

DATE

WHY I'M GRATEFUL TODAY, MORE OR LESS:

TODAY'S GRATITUDE LEVEL: